Who Dies Wins

A comedy thriller

Seymour Matthews

Samuel French — London
New York - Toronto - Hollywood

WHO DIES WINS

First produced under the title **BODY OF EVIDENCE** by
Jack Watling Productions at the Frinton Summer Theatre
on 10th August 1999 with the following cast:

Léon Winter	Guy Michaels
Abby Winter	Jane Colenutt
Raymond Brown	Barnaby Edwards
Sophie Brown	Kathryn Tennant Maw
John Drummond	James Hirst
Molly Drummond	Juliet Warner
Chief Inspector Norbert Plum	Seymour Matthews
Detective Sergeant	Mark Holman
Piers Gerard	George Spelvin

Directed and designed by Seymour Matthews

CHARACTERS

Léon Winter; forty (see Author's Note)
Abby Winter; mid-thirties
Raymond Brown; forty
Sophie Brown; late thirties
John Drummond; thirty
Molly Drummond; thirty
Chief Inspector Norbert Plum; mid-fifties
Piers Gerard; thirty-five
Detective Constable (male or female, preferably female)

The action takes place in the lounge area of Léon and Abby Winter's substantial detached property outside Banbury in Oxfordshire

SYNOPSIS OF SCENES

ACT I   A Friday evening in October
               Approximately 7.20 p.m.

ACT II
    Scene 1   Five days later. Late afternoon
    Scene 2   Immediately following

Time — the present

AUTHOR'S NOTES

Léon and Piers

It is absolutely essential that the opening scene between Abby and Piers (her lover) appears to the audience as a scene between Abby and Léon (her husband). There is no attempt by Piers to impersonate Léon until the other guests arrive; Piers is simply being himself but the audience must *think* he is Léon. To help the actors achieve this, the dialogue of the entire scene is deliberately constructed to have a double meaning. And to intensify this deception, they should appear to be plotting nothing more sinister than — *a practical joke!*

It is not until Piers' entrance in Act II that the audience realize their mistake (hopefully!). In the opening scene, while he is alone with Abby, Piers is his real self and decidedly masculine, whereas when he returns at the end of Act I and throughout Act II he adopts a Californian accent and a mildly fey and rather camp persona. Léon, in fact, never appears, the reason for which becomes apparent towards the end of the play.

To assist in this deception of the audience, the character Léon Winter should appear on the cast list in all theatre programmes. A suitably fictitious actor's name should also appear alongside it. This is an established theatrical convention (i.e. in *Sleuth,* etc.). The most commonly used name for the actor is Walter Plinge, though the name Noel Trewin might be appropriate as it is an anagram of Léon Winter. I leave it up to the director's discretion.

The taped voice — ACT I

The taped voice in ACT I, impersonating Hercule Poirot, is that of the real Léon Winter.

Vansittart

I like to think that Plum's pronunciation of this name, "Fancy tart", is very much what Léon — the practical joker — intended.

Seymour Matthews

Other plays by Seymour Matthews
published by Samuel French Ltd

Anagram of Murder
Dead Man's Hand

ACT I

The lounge area of Léon and Abby Winter's substantial detached property outside Banbury in Oxfordshire. A Friday evening in September, approximately 7.20 p.m.

The essential components of the stage area are as follows. There is a door to the study R with an archway UR leading to the front door and the rest of the house. UL there is a large window which overlooks the driveway, indicating that the house is set back from the road. There is a door L which leads to a lobby; this leads to the kitchen

The décor and furnishings are expensive and tasteful; these include a drinks cabinet, on which, among other things, are bottles of mineral water, gin, tonic, whisky and an opened bottle of white wine in a cooler. There are various prints and paintings around the walls, most of them rather bizarre. On one wall is a framed print which is completely black. There is a telephone on a table below the window and elsewhere there is a hi-fi and speakers

When the CURTAIN *rises the stage is empty and we hear classical music playing softly in the kitchen. The lighting is subdued*

After a moment Piers enters from the kitchen. He is an ageing thirty-something wearing an apron and yellow washing-up gloves. He helps himself to a drink of mineral water, moves to the framed black painting and raises his glass to it

(See Author's Note p.vi)

Piers OK Alphonse — let's make the people laugh!

The phone rings. Piers heads for the phone

   Abby enters from the study. She is also in her late thirties

The two of them are very playful, on a high — a mixture of exultation and fear

Abby Don't you even think about it! (*She shoos him away from the phone and picks up the receiver*) Four — five —three — three. … Mother!

(*Irritated by this interruption*) How lovely to hear from you. ... He's what? ... Has he, indeed? Why don't you call the Citizens' Advice people? ... Or Relate? ... Relate, Mother! You probably still call it the Marriage Guidance Bureau. ... Oh, you're not married to him ... Well, I thought you were. It makes me a bit of a bastard, if you're not, doesn't it? ... Look, I don't care if you have shouted "I divorce you!" three times through the bedroom keyhole, that only works if you're in Damascus. ... Well, maybe it's his time of month; have you got a full moon down there tonight? ... Yes, Mother, Léon is here. (*She looks at Piers playfully*) ... He's preparing one of his fabulous dinner parties, we're having some friends over. ... But Mother, we do invite you, it's just that you're both so far away. ... Yes, he's standing right across the room from me. Would you like to speak to him? (*She holds the phone out to Piers*)

Piers retreats across the room

Oh, he's had to dash back into the kitchen — what a shame. ... Maybe next time, Moth ... Oh, she's rung off. (*She hangs up. To Piers*) You've been saved by the bell. Honestly, I could've happily murdered my parents years ago.

Piers So why didn't you?

Abby They always seem to be on the verge of murdering each other — I thought they'd do it for me, save me the trouble. I'm still waiting.

Piers Forget about them. They're thousands of miles away. (*He advances on her*)

Abby (*restraining him, gently*) There's no time for that. You're supposed to be preparing a delectable meal, remember?

Piers Oh, that particular delectable dish can wait. I've got my eyes on another one, after — you know what. Don't you find it has that effect on you? (*He moves to put an arm around her waist*)

Abby (*avoiding his embrace*) Even if it did, our guests will be arriving any minute. You might at least try and behave like a gourmet chef.

Piers Who said I was a gourmet chef?

Abby You did, remember? You do — endlessly ... Remember?

Piers (*sarcastically*) Oh, yes. How could I forget. Well, they won't be here for five minutes.

Abby Oh, charming; is that all the time you need?

Piers moves to kiss her

(*Avoiding him again*) No! I am not making love to you in rubber gloves and an apron — anyway, we may have forgotten something!

Piers (*in a cod Italian accent*) I have forgotten nothing, signora. All is prepared to perfection.

Abby I wasn't referring to the food.

Piers Neither was I.

Abby You know precisely what I meant.

Piers Everything is ready.

Abby What if ... (*She pauses*) Well, what if Ray and Sophie don't get here first?

Piers Ray will be on time — he always is. He's a creature of habit.

Abby What if John's early?

Piers No chance.

Abby What if he comes in the wrong car? What if they actually arrive here in the Range Rover?

Piers They won't.

Abby What if he changes the wheel?

Piers Abby ... ! John's too darned lazy ... Anyway, he wouldn't know how to. Look, it's going to be a fantastic evening. It'll go like clockwork. It has done so far. All you have to do is keep them out of the kitchen while I'm being — "creative".

Abby What if Molly twigs the whole thing? She might spill the beans.

Piers I hardly think so. I know she's one of your dearest friends, but she's always been a couple of sandwiches short of a picnic.

Abby He might not have told Molly anything — he might have kept it to himself.

Piers John is incapable of keeping mum about anything — he's hopeless at keeping secrets of any kind. (*Sarcastically*) I should know — he tells *me* everything.

Abby (*equally sarcastically*) Oh, yes. How could I forget. (*She smiles*)

There is a pause

(*Relaxing a little*) I can't wait to be rid of him — completely.

Piers Angel, a few hours more and we will be — for good.

Abby I keep thinking of those seven days in the Lake District ... They were idyllic ...

Piers As from tomorrow everything will be idyllic.

Abby And that weekend in Stroud ... Paradise ...

Piers laughs

What's funny?

Piers I never thought a weekend in Stroud could ever be called paradise ...

They both laugh softly

But I know what you mean ...

Abby I don't want anything or anybody to come between us ever again ...

Piers After tonight nobody will come between us; just keep focused on that Abby. Not him — or anyone else ... Never again ... (*He moves to kiss her*)

Abby (*avoiding him*) Shouldn't you be busy in the kitchen ... ?

Piers Everything is on schedule ... I do know what I'm doing, you know. Anyone would think I'd never done this before ...

Abby But you have — of course you have ... You're the master craftsman ...

Piers I like to think so ...

Abby I'm sorry. I'm worrying about nothing. I know how meticulous you are. How could I ever doubt you'd remember everything down to the minutest detail.

Piers You flatter me.

Abby Not at all, you are the chef — and this will be your *chef-d'oeuvre* — your masterpiece ...

Piers You forget, I'm just following the recipe — it's your masterpiece ...

Abby Now you're flattering *me*; let's just say it's *our* masterpiece.

They kiss very gently

I feel as if I'm on some kind of drug ... It's been injected directly into my veins and shot straight to my brain; it heightens all your senses — don't you feel it?

Piers Abby, come on down. The evening has only just begun — we've a long way to go yet before we're back in paradise ...

Abby (*smiling*) Back in Stroud, you mean?

Piers (*smiling*) Yes, back in Stroud ... You know, I can't believe that old car of mine ever made it up that hill. By the time we got to the top the power had completely gone; we just free-wheeled it into that car-park and then the bonnet literally exploded ...

Abby And we had to stay three days while they repaired it ...

Piers What a terrible inconvenience that was ...

Abby (*leading him on*) It wasn't the only thing that exploded that weekend, I can tell you. It was like a voyage of discovery ... For one thing, I recognized the real man I'd been married to all these years.

Piers And what did you see?

Abby It was a revelation — pure serendipity. I always knew my life would have a happy ending.

Piers I don't want your life to have a happy ending.

Abby Why not?

Piers Because if you have a happy life then the ending of it would be very sad. Only if you had a miserable life would the ending of it be happy.

Abby You know what I mean.

Piers I always know what you mean. (*He moves towards her again*)

Abby Ah, ah, remember — let's stick to the task in hand. Shouldn't you be peeling something or other?

Piers Peeling something? Abby, please … I shall be shaping a work of art, a creation to deceive the eye and — well, maybe the palate as well, who knows?

Abby (*laughing*) I hope it doesn't get that far.

Piers I think this calls for a celebratory drink. A toast to our enterprise.

Abby Just a small one, darling, you're driving tonight.

Piers I meant mineral water; we can't take any risks. And I must remember to pour the Taylor's Reserve down the sink.

Abby (*playfully*) You sneak! You said you'd forgotten nothing — you said everything was prepared to perfection.

Piers So I lied!

Abby You ——

Piers No, no, no — I'm pulling your leg, it's already done, I promise you. So; a toast … (*He hands her a glass*)

Abby A toast …

Piers (*as an obvious quote*) "Never forget — the idea of a practical joke is to make people laugh."

They smile and drink. The phone rings again. Abby answers it

Abby (*into the phone*) Four — five … Mother. … What's he done this time?

Piers exits casually through the kitchen door

He's chopped off the heads of your what? … I see. … Your rhododendrons. Well … Why don't you chop off something of his? … I wasn't particularly thinking of the garden, Mother.

Headlights appear through the window

Look, Mother, I'm having a dinner party and my first guests have arrived. I really must go. … (*In exasperation*) Well, ring the Fire Brigade! (*She hangs up*)

Piers reappears in the doorway

It's Sophie and Raymond. Precisely on time — as you said they would be.

Piers Right!

Abby You're sure everything's ready?

Piers As ready as we'll ever be!

Abby Here's to a successful dinner party!

Piers The hors-d'œuvres went down well — now let's see about the main course; this is going to be "Léon Winter's *pièce de résistance*". And remember ... (*he smiles*) whatever you do, keep your odious friends out of my kitchen!

Piers exits to the kitchen and closes the door

Abby moves to the hall, turning on more lights as she goes. She exits

We hear the front door opening

Abby (*off, switching effortlessly to "hostess" mode*) Sophie, darling, how lovely to see you. Raymond, do come in. It's so long since we've seen you both ——

Abby, Raymond and Sophie enter. Abby is ahead of the other two. Raymond and Sophie are very much the life and soul of any dinner party; they are always first on anyone's list. Their verbal sparring is all very good-natured. They are both sun-tanned

Abby heads straight for the kitchen door

— we want to hear everything. I'm just packing Léon off to the off-licence; we've forgotten the port for John, I'm afraid.

Raymond Oh dear — that'll never do. I'll go with him if you like. Keep him company.

Abby You'll do no such thing. You'll end up in the pub, the two of you; I know you of old. You get Sophie a drink and behave yourself; you know where they're kept.

Abby exits into the kitchen

We hear Piers expertly "chopping"

(*Off*) I should just get the best port you can find, darling.

The kitchen door closes

Raymond Spritzer, as usual?

Sophie Do I ever drink anything else?

Raymond helps himself to the white wine. He makes a spritzer and hands it to Sophie during the following

Raymond Looks like Léon is preparing one of his special dinners again. He spends all day in that kitchen, sometimes.

Sophie Which is more than I can say for you, my darling.

Raymond But is it really necessary?

Sophie Well, the results are usually pretty spectacular.

Raymond Oh, I'm not complaining — he's a great cook. But he does get a bit uptight about the whole thing; everything has to be just right, you know.

Sophie He's a perfectionist — I admire that in a man.

Raymond I dare say I'd admire it in a woman, if I ever came across it.

Sophie Do you remember that time at their old house, when we all sat around for an hour between courses?

Raymond Oh, my God, what a disaster that was. And all for a plate of overdone steak and chips.

Sophie I mean, the soup was absolutely gorgeous but it was so obvious that what they'd planned for the main course had gone disastrously wrong and they rustled up the steaks as a last resort.

Raymond I wouldn't have minded but they carried on as if nothing had happened — no apology for keeping us waiting. They both behaved as if they'd been gone two minutes and everything was hunky-dory.

Sophie You know, I've often wondered if that whole evening wasn't one of Léon's excruciating con-tricks.

Raymond I doubt it. Léon always says: " … the idea of a practical joke is to make people laugh." If that evening was one of them then it died a death.

Sophie It did rather go down like a lead balloon.

Raymond Yes …

Sophie The worst thing was being left alone for a whole hour with that dreadful couple from the library.

Raymond She was from the library; he was an undertaker, I think.

Sophie Well, he certainly bored me to death …

Raymond makes himself a gin and tonic during the following

We hear the sound of a food mixer coming from the kitchen

Sophie Am I imagining things or can I smell burning? Don't tell me Léon has done the unthinkable …

Raymond Don't be ridiculous. There doesn't appear to be any ice. (*He moves towards the kitchen door*)

Sophie I wouldn't go in there — not while the maestro is at work … You know what Léon's like.

Raymond reaches the door

> *The door opens. Abby enters carrying an ice bucket and stands in the doorway*

Abby Ice — I nearly forgot.

Abby gives the ice bucket to Raymond

Raymond Thanks. (*He calls through the open door*) If you need any expert advice, old boy, I'm available!

The food mixer sound stops

Piers (*off*) Ha, ha!

Raymond takes the ice back to the drinks

Abby (*turning in the doorway*) Have you got enough money, Léon?
Piers (*off*) Yeah.
Abby Be quick as you can.
Piers (*off*) OK.

The phone rings. Abby closes the kitchen door and answers the phone

Abby (*into the phone*) Four — five — three — three. ... Good eve ... Molly! ... What's wrong, darling? Why aren't you here? ... Oh, no. ... Oh, Molly. ... How infuriating. ... A puncture, you say? ... John's changing the what? ... Well, why don't you come in your ... ? Yes, that's a good idea, I was going to suggest that. Otherwise you'd miss the first course and that would never do. ... Léon would be mortally wounded. ... You know what he's like about punctuality; he'll serve the meal at eight whether you're here or not. ... Yes, you can sort it all out tomorrow. Don't worry, Molly — there'll be a drink here waiting for you. Bye. (*She puts the phone down*) Can you believe it? They were just about to drive off ... discovered they had a puncture. They're coming in Molly's car. They shouldn't be long.

We hear the sound of Léon's Range Rover driving away. Abby waves out of the window

Sophie Abby ... am I hallucinating, or can I smell burning coming from the kitchen?
Abby Burning?

Sophie Has King Alfred burnt the cakes?

Abby Oh, that ... No, no, that was me. A little accident with the melba toast for the first course.

Raymond A bit early for the first course, isn't it? We're the only ones here ...

Abby Oh, it was only a dry run ... Just as well, really — the master would've scolded me had it been the real thing ...

Sophie My dear, I believe you. Hung, drawn and quartered, more like. Well, now we've got you alone, what's on the menu for tonight?

Abby I'm sworn to secrecy, you know that. He'd sulk for a week if he knew I'd told you.

Raymond Oh, come on, Abby. We're dying to know.

Abby I can't possibly tell you.

Raymond Can't you give us a clue? Please?

Abby Ray — you're incorrigible.

Sophie Abby — you'll have to tell him eventually. He's like a dog with a bone. He won't stop till you give in.

A pause

Abby Oh, all right. But you're not to breathe a word, either of you.

Sophie We promise.

Raymond Cross my heart and hope to die!

Abby It's a recipe he picked up in Venice in the Spring ...

Sophie I don't remember Léon going to Venice ...

Raymond Of course you do, darling; he sent us that postcard: "Arrived safely. Streets flooded. Please advise."

Sophie Oh, yes, very droll.

Abby And it just happens to be Ray's favourite kind of dish ...

Sophie Oh, what — sauerkraut?

Raymond Isn't she delightful? Do I detect something "fishy" going on here?

Abby You do indeed — it's called meagre; meagre baked in champagne with caviar cream sauce.

Raymond Caviar cream ... ? Oh, sounds wonderful ...

Sophie What on earth's meagre?

Abby Some kind of sea bass — I think it's found in Australia or somewhere. But not a word to Léon.

Raymond An Aussie fish dish — I can't wait. (*With a "cod" Aussie accent*) "Perhaps with a perky little Chardonnay from South Billabong to wash it down with, eh? As Sir Les Patterson said to me last night in the gents ... "

Sophie Ray — please ... not now ...

Raymond (*Aussie accent*) "I was just telling a joke, sweetheart."

Sophie Yes, but not that one — (*distastefully*) it's disgusting!

Raymond (*Aussie accent*) "Anything you say, Sheila."
Sophie Sophie, if you don't mind …
Raymond (*dropping the accent*) Yes, dear, anything you say, dear. Abby, can I fix you a drink?
Abby No, thanks, I've got one in the kitchen, but do help yourselves, please.

Raymond tops up Sophie's drink and his own

Sophie Just the six of us tonight, is it?
Abby And Piers …
Raymond Oh, no, not that creep.
Abby Now Ray, he's perfectly charming, and quite harmless.
Raymond He may be harmless to you ladies, but to me … Well, I feel distinctly uneasy whenever he's around.
Sophie Oh, darling, I hardly think he'd fancy you, even if you were the last man on the planet; you're not his type.
Raymond And just what is his "type"?
Sophie Someone whose IQ is bigger than his waistline, I should think.
Abby Now, now you two — you happen to be talking about a very good friend of mine.
Raymond You've only known him a few months.
Abby So? He makes me laugh. He's interested in books, the theatre, movies … He's damned good company and you know it.
Sophie Apparently he's joined the local amateur dramatic group. According to Marjorie, when he's acting he's butcher than all the other men put together.
Raymond As the only other male actor in the group is Marjorie's husband that's not exactly saying much, is it?
Sophie They're putting on *Rebecca* by Daphne du Maurier at the end of the month. Piers is playing Maxim de Winter.
Raymond You're kidding!
Sophie No, it's true. And guess who's playing Mrs de Winter!
Abby That girl from the boutique, isn't it?
Raymond What, Belinda Martin?
Sophie As I live and breathe: right little tart, she is! And according to Marjorie, their love scenes together are … Well …
Abby What do you mean?
Sophie Well … !
Raymond ⎫
        ⎬ (*together*) According to Marjorie ——
Sophie ⎭
Sophie — if Piers is gay — then he must be a very, very good actor.
Raymond You mean Piers and Belinda are ——
Sophie Say no more, my darling, say no more …

Abby There's no reason why he shouldn't be a good actor; he was a professional, at one time.

Raymond Piers — a professional actor?

Abby Apparently. For about ten years — so he said — in California. But he never made a go of it, so he came over here and drifted into antiques.

Sophie And — according to Marjorie — his English accent is impeccable.

Raymond So, our precious Piers is going to be Maxim de Winter. (*In a W. C. Fields voice*) "Maxim D. Winter from the US of A." Maybe they're distant relations of yours, Abby!

Abby Mm?

Raymond De Winter ... Winter?

Abby (*laughing*) Oh, heavens ... I doubt it, somehow.

Raymond (*to Sophie*) You should have volunteered to play Mrs Danvers, darling — but then I know how you hate being typecast.

Sophie (*giving Raymond a withering look*) Why don't we all go and see it? It might be fun.

Abby I've already got my tickets — front row on the opening night. Piers got them for me.

Raymond I think a little bird told him you write the reviews for the local rag and he's trying to butter you up beforehand ...

Abby No. He just wants me there — to support him. Anyway, I don't write them any more. Not since last year when Léon and that playwright ... Well ...

Sophie Oh, darling, don't remind me, how embarrassing. I always knew Léon's wicked sense of humour would rebound on him one day. Still, I understand the poor man made a full recovery. I felt sorry for him, really — I mean, his wife was an absolute gorgon.

Raymond Oh well, if you're going to talk about me ... I'm on call, Abby, do you mind if I phone the desk — tell them where I am?

Abby No, no, of course not.

Raymond moves to the phone and makes a call during the following

Sophie Personally, darling, I'm delighted Piers is coming — gives me something to ogle at. He may be gay, but I think it's criminal — such a waste.

Abby Sophie — really. (*She nods towards Raymond*)

Sophie Oh, Ray doesn't care; he doesn't mind me window-shopping, as long as I don't buy.

Raymond Hi, it's Ray Brown, put me through to the news desk, will you?

There is a moment's pause. Abby looks fleetingly at her watch

Raymond (*into the phone*) Gerry, it's Ray, anything happening? (*He mimes a conversation during the following*)
Sophie Abby, what is it?
Abby Uh … ?
Sophie There's something on your mind, I can tell. What is it?
Abby No, no, I'm fine, honestly.
Sophie Darling, this is Sophie, remember? Might do you good to talk about it. Is it Léon again?
Abby No, no, Léon's been a sweetie … Things are so much better since we went away. No, it's work, that's all.

Sophie looks quizzically at Abby

I'm working on Harrison Baker's new novel. It's the first one I've done of his. Marilyn Peters did the others but she retired last Christmas and this one's fallen to me.
Sophie You should be honoured; he's a terrific writer.
Abby I am. And he is. But I don't think this one is up to his usual standard. I've suggested some rewrites but so far he's pooh-poohed the lot of them. He's come up with a second draft but it's virtually identical to the first. The thing is, do I stand my ground and antagonize him — he's very powerful, you know — or do I cave in and risk a failure with the critics?

Raymond puts the phone down

Sophie Abby, no editor ever kept her integrity by giving in to a writer.
Raymond Nor her virginity, come to that.
Sophie Ray, please.
Abby I know what I have to do, really; it's just that — will the directors back me?
Sophie Well, they damn well ought to, that's all I can say. You're one of the best editors there is. Still, I guess there's only one way to find out.
Abby Yes, you're right. (*She deliberately changes the subject*) But we're not here to talk shop. Now — I want to hear all about your trip across the "Pond".
Sophie That's history now, we've been back a fortnight.
Abby But I haven't seen you, you're always so busy.
Sophie Well — the weather was fantastic.
Raymond In the entire three weeks it never dipped below eighty degrees, hardly ever below ninety and three times it topped a hundred. One Sunday it reached a hundred and eight Fahrenheit.
Abby How marvellous!
Raymond And it's a very dry heat — no humidity. You don't sweat nearly so much as you do in the tropics.

Sophie Did you know there are thirty-two miles of beaches in Los Angeles? Ray and I must have walked or cycled every single one of them.

Abby I can't imagine Ray on a bicycle!

Raymond Only way to travel on the beaches, old girl. Flat as a pancake everywhere, miles and miles of bike paths, cool sea breezes ... Wonderful!

Abby Did you go to Malibu and Santa Monica?

Raymond Is the Pope Catholic?

Abby And Long Beach?

Sophie Yes, but they're for the tourists.

Abby You two were tourists.

Sophie Abby, please ... We were "visitors".

Raymond I think my favourite has to be Venice Beach. What an experience; it's a sort of throwback to the seventies. Hippies everywhere; masses of stalls selling everything you can think of: clothes, food; you could have your photo taken with a snake or a cockatoo; body-piercing; tattooing; some guy making sand-sculptures ...

Sophie And next to it was Muscle Beach ... Lots of budding Arnold Schwartzeneggers pumping iron ... All those bronzed bodies, darling.

Raymond I was leaning on the rail watching these guys doing their jerk and snatch or whatever it is they do, when this pectorally-challenged midget put down his dumb-bells, sidled up to me and said, (*in his best American accent*) "You know, I've always wondered what Johnny Weissmuller did in those Tarzan films when Jane wasn't around ..."

Abby What did you say?

Raymond I said, "It's never troubled me, duckie ..." and I pedalled away as fast as I could.

Sophie Only in California!

Raymond Too right. But the most amazing thing to me was the price of everything: it was so incredibly cheap! Not that we're short of a bob or two — I mean, I'm used to my darling wife keeping me in the manner to which I am accustomed — but over there in Chinatown you can get a seriously good take-away for three dollars fifty, which is about two pounds twelve p. And we found this hostelry which had two hundred and fifty different beers on draught ...

Sophie (*distastefully*) You mean you found it!

Raymond The bar was about forty feet long, then it turned the corner and came back again another forty feet, beer pumps all the way round, continuously. It had Theakston's draught "Old Peculier" — I was in seventh heaven, wasn't I, darling?

Sophie Continuously — and very peculiar ...

Raymond And you know California is full of batty religious cults ... ? Well, we came across this group that worship snack foods; they have a particular reverence for "Cheesits" — you know, those little packets of cheese biscuits, "Cheesits? — they call them "The Snackrament" — it's true, I swear it — and their favourite hymn is — wait for it — "What a friend we have in Cheesits" ...

The women laugh merrily

You think I'm joking — but I'm not. It's perfectly true. Léon would have been in his element.

Abby You must tell him all about it.

Sophie I'm afraid Ray was like a schoolboy who'd found a box of Dinky toys ...

Abby You obviously both had a wonderful time ...

Raymond I think you can safely say that we did ...

Sophie (*to Raymond*) All quiet on the Western Front?

Raymond Mm? Oh, back at the factory? Yes, fine. We're waiting for a Government Minister to resign, but that's old hat these days — hardly headline material. No, it's deadly quiet, I'm afraid — unless we get a nice juicy Home Counties murder. You and Léon aren't planning on poisoning us all tonight, are you Abby, by any chance?

Abby Ray, please, credit me with a little more subtlety.

Raymond Yes, that's what I thought ... Shame.

Sophie Abby, is there anything we can do to help? Lay the table or something?

Abby It's all done. Don't worry.

Raymond Shall I open some wine? Let it breathe ... I do know where you keep it.

Abby Everything's in hand, Ray. If you start interfering with Léon's dinner party he'll hit the roof, you know he will. He'll get ratty with everybody and take it out on me for a week.

There is a sudden Black-out. Every light goes out. The music from the kitchen stops

Sophie Oh, my God!
Raymond What's happened?

A pause

Raymond Abby — are you there?
Abby Yes — yes, of course I'm here ...
Sophie Well, what is it? A power cut?
Abby I — I don't know.
Raymond Maybe it's a fuse.
Sophie It would happen when Léon's out of the house, wouldn't it? Ray's useless in the dark; he can't even undo a bra-strap.

Raymond Do you have a torch anywhere, Abby?
Abby Yes ... There's one in the hall cupboard — where we hang the coats.
Raymond I'll go ...

Raymond feels his way out to the hall

Abby The fuse box is in there too, Ray.

A pause

I think there's some candles in the kitchen ... I'll have a look.

Abby feels her way towards the kitchen

Sophie Oh, don't leave me alone, Abby!
Abby I shan't be long, Sophie.

Abby exits

There is a long pause

Sophie (*very nervously*) Ray ... Ray ...

A pause

Oh dear — now where did I put my ...

A pause. We hear Sophie moving about for a while; then, suddenly, she screams

Raymond enters carrying a torch and a larger light source like a battery-operated storm lamp

Raymond Darling ... You OK, old girl?
Sophie Sorry — I went to take a sip of my drink and spilt some on my arm.

Abby enters from the kitchen with a candle

Abby Sophie, what is it?
Sophie False alarm, I'm afraid.
Abby I managed to find one candle, but that's all there is. Did you check the fuse box, Ray?
Raymond No, I'd just found the flashlights when Sophie screamed. I'll go back and look. Here, I'll leave this one with you.

Raymond exits once more, leaving one of the torches with the women

Sophie Sorry about the hysterics. I never have liked the dark — ever since I was a little girl.

Abby That's OK, Soph …

Sophie It always scared me rigid. I remember standing in the hallway of our old house one night, just Tony and me, my brother — we were waiting for Daddy to come back from a business trip abroad … It was his birthday … It was very late and very dark. We just stood staring out the window in complete silence. Suddenly we both turned and looked up the stairs behind us, then at each other and then scarpered to the other end of the house up the other staircase and into Mummy's room. We'd neither of us seen or heard anything — but we just knew there was somebody standing on the stairs … We both sensed — a presence. Scary! I was only eight.

Abby You don't believe in ghosts, surely?

Sophie Absolutely! Too right I do! Me and Léon both. We often compare spooks …

Abby Well, I hope we don't see any tonight. There's only enough food for seven.

Sophie What about the food; won't it spoil? If we can't restore the power it really will be a "meagre" offering.

Abby No problem — the Aga's solid fuel. But it won't be much fun eating it in the dark.

Sophie Oh, I don't know. A candlelit dinner — could be frightfully romantic …

Abby I'm not sure I'm feeling terribly romantic — at the moment.

Sophie We might even conjure up a gay ghost for Piers …

Raymond enters from the hall carrying a note

Raymond Well, I checked the fuses — they all seem OK. But … I did find this — taped to the fuse box. (*He hands the note to the women*)

Abby (*reading*) "Now is the winter …"

Sophie Oh no …

Raymond Exactly!

Sophie Not Léon fooling around again — please!

Abby is clearly dumbstruck by the note

Raymond That's what it looks like. What else could it be?

Abby (*softly*) I don't believe this …

Sophie Did you know anything about this, Abby?

Abby No, no … (*Genuinely*) I assure you this has come as a complete surprise to me …

Sophie How could he have switched off the lights if he wasn't even here?

Raymond Oh, you know Léon and his gadgets. He would have found a way, believe you me. It's not beyond the powers of his imagination to arrange a power cut. This is obviously one of his games and we now have to play it out. His trip to the off-licence was obviously pre-planned. He must have turned off the lights by remote control — or some sort of timer, more likely.

Sophie Well, I suppose we might as well sit back and enjoy it. We usually end up having a good laugh at Léon's antics.

Raymond As long as I get fed, I don't mind. I'm getting mighty hungry.

Sophie Don't worry, my pet. The cooker's not electric so your precious dinner is perfectly safe.

Abby That's right. I can't see Léon sacrificing one of his culinary masterpieces — not even for a practical joke. I'm sure it's still simmering gently away. (*She glances towards the kitchen*)

Another set of headlights appears through the window

Raymond Is that Léon back already?

Abby I think that's probably Molly and John.

Abby picks up one of the torches. She puts the note down, moves to the window and shines the torch through the glass

Yes it is. Would you let them in while I check the food? (*She flashes the torch once or twice through the window*)

Sophie I'll go.

Abby closes the curtains and exits to the kitchen, closing the door behind her

Sophie takes the other torch and exits to the front door

We hear the front door open

Raymond takes the opportunity to top up his gin by candlelight. He also pours a Scotch for John

Sophie (*off*) Hi Molly, John! Come on in.

Molly (*off*) Hello, Sophie.

John (*off*) What's going on? It's not Hallowe'en yet, you know. Have you blown a fuse or what?

Sophie enters guiding John and Molly Drummond by torchlight. John is a typical "Essex Man" made good, a bit of a rough diamond. His wife is a middle-class mouse, but a pretty one

Sophie Something like that.

John I was beginning to think you'd stood us up and gone out.

Sophie We're a couple of drinks ahead of you, I'm afraid.

John Don't worry, I'll catch you up in five minutes flat. Just get me a large Scotch, will you — neat.

Raymond hands John the Scotch he has just poured

Well, where's the happy couple?

Molly Johnny!

John Léon poking his nose in the fuse-box, is he?

Raymond Abby's in the kitchen, Léon's gone to the off-licence ostensibly to get you a decent port!

John Oh, I see. You're all waiting for Mr Fix-It here to roll up his sleeves and get stuck in, is that it?

Raymond Not exactly! The lights went out after Léon had left but we found this taped to the fuse-box. (*He picks up the note and hands it to John*)

John (*reading*) "Now is the winter …?"

Molly (*with a light smile*) Oh, not again — not tonight … Please …

Sophie I'm afraid so …

Raymond We think he must have rigged up a timer to switch off the electricity while he was out. It's obviously his little game; we'll just have to grin and bear it.

John Well, that's no problem. Where's the mains switch? I'll soon sort that out.

Raymond Now just a minute, John. If you turn the lights back on and spoil Léon's cabaret for the evening then he's not going to be a happy bunny, is he?

John But I could fix it easily.

Sophie I dare say you could, John, but Ray does have a point. When all's said and done, we always have a good laugh at these things. We humour Léon for a while, we get a slap-up meal and drink ourselves legless. What more could you want?

John Yeah … I suppose so.

Molly And you get a bottle of port to yourself, John!

Raymond Well said, Molly! Look, it's Abby's party. She's as much in the dark about this as the rest of us. We'll do what she wants.

Sophie Ray's right. Let me get you a spritzer, Molly, cheer you up.

Molly Thanks, Sophie.

Raymond Bad luck about the puncture, old man.

John That's just it. It wasn't a puncture. Some hooligan had actually stuck a knife into the tyre and ripped a three-inch gash — can you believe it?

The following is all good-hearted banter, nothing too serious

Raymond Well, if you will live opposite the Grindley Estate, old bean, what do you expect?

Sophie Ray, please.

John Damn council estate. They're all vandals. If I catch them at it …

Raymond I know, I know — you'll castrate the lot of them. Are you sure you haven't rubbed somebody up the wrong way over there?

John Who me? I've never said a word to anyone on that estate. Ever.

Raymond Maybe that's why …

John Now come on, Ray — I do my bit for the community but I draw the line at fraternizing with that lot.

Raymond I hardly think being Chairman of the local Neighbourhood Watch red-necks qualifies as "doing your bit for the community". Bringing back the birch is not going to rid the leafy glades of Oxfordshire of vandalism.

John I suppose your brand of Liberal Democrat would bang them up in some cosy detention centre, rent free, with a TV in every cell and room service provided by the Spice Girls …

Sophie Now that's enough, you two …

John Well, what kind of low-life would slash a car tyre just for the sheer hell of it?

Sophie John, if you will park a brand new Range Rover a hundred yards from that estate …

John I should be able to park outside my own front door …

Abby enters with another bottle of wine and some canapés

Abby Molly …

Molly Hi, Abby …

Abby I'm sorry about this, people — Léon's up to his tricks again, I'm afraid.

John Abby, if you want, I could have your lights working in two minutes flat …

Abby (*quite keen*) Oh, do you think you could, John?

John Just point me to the mains switch … Where is it, in the kitchen? (*He takes a step toward the kitchen door*)

Abby puts a hand up to stop John; he stops

Molly We were just saying, Abby: assuming this is Léon up to his usual shenanigans, if we fix the lights before he comes back, he's not going to be too pleased, is he?

Raymond Unless that's part of the game ——

Everyone looks at Raymond

— that we fix the lights ourselves?

Abby I see what you mean …

Suddenly a recorded voice comes from the hi-fi speakers. The voice is a very passable imitation of Hercule Poirot from the TV series; it is therefore soft, breathy and very French. It is not obviously recognizable as Léon except to those present in the room, who know him well

Voice Good-evening! *Bon soir, Mesdames et Messieurs!*

Everyone reacts

I have been asked by Monsieur Léon Winter to welcome you to his little soirée — in the dark! But not to worry — it is only temporary … Normal service will be resumed shortly.

The guests react with varying degrees of amusement. Abby listens intently

No doubt your guests have arrived to keep you company, Madame Winter and, I dare say, by now you have retrieved the flashlights from the hall cupboard. But what about the fuse-box … You may find something there to your advantage, a little pointer as to where this evening will be leading us. My services have been engaged by Monsieur Winter to help you unravel the mystery. So let us apply our little grey cells and see how much of the clue you can solve before he returns. As soon as this tape finishes you will be in for a pleasant surprise. *Au revoir* — for now — *mes amis!*
John (*chuckling*) Oh boy! Where does he drag them up from …

All the lights come on again. The music resumes playing softly in the kitchen

All (*severally*) Whoah! Let there be light! Good old Léon! Thank goodness for that! So much for our candlelit dinner. (*Etc.*)
Abby (*somewhat relieved*) Well — who's for another drink?
John Yes, why not? It might help lubricate the little grey cells.

Everyone gets another drink. Torches are switched off and the candle is blown out

Raymond So — what is this clue we've got to "unravel"? "Now is the winter …"
Sophie Well, it's a quotation isn't it? Shakespeare … *Richard III*, I think …
John Not another of his Shakespearean riddles …
Sophie "Now is the winter — of our discontent — Made glorious summer — by this son of York …" Or something like that.

John I say, Soph, you're not just a pretty face after all …

Raymond But what does it mean … ?

Sophie Not the foggiest, I'm afraid … Some sort of "play" on his name — Winter — I suppose …

Abby (*changing the subject*) I'm so glad you made it, Molly. But what a time to get a puncture.

John Oh, it's nothing … These things happen.

Raymond John says the puncture may have been vandalism — hooligans from the estate …

Abby Oh, no, how awful.

Molly I still say it could be whoever wrote the letters …

John Molly, please …

Sophie What letters?

Molly Why don't you tell them, John?

Abby Tell us what?

Molly About the letters!

Sophie What letters?

John Just a couple of threatening letters from some nutter — it was nothing.

Molly He threatened to kill you. I don't call that nothing!

John (*trying to keep the conversation light*) Molly, please. I don't want to go through all that again. We're here to have a nice quiet dinner with our friends, OK?

Sophie (*eager for some new gossip*) Now hang on a minute … what's all this about threatening to kill you? It sounds a mite serious to me.

Molly John has received two anonymous letters in the past week. I think it's someone he owes money to, but he won't admit it to me.

John Molly …

Molly John, these are our closest friends. Who else do we confide in? You won't go to the police.

Raymond If you'd like me to take a look at them …

John Look … I appreciate you're trying to help — all of you — but I do have an idea who this is.

The others all look at John, forcing him to elaborate a little

I've been doing some business with a guy named Vansittart …

Abby reacts slightly on hearing this name

I think it's him, and I know how to handle it — really! I don't know about you, but I've had a hard day. Don't let it spoil our evening, eh?

Raymond OK.

Sophie Molly?

Molly OK … OK … Let's forget about it — for tonight, anyway.

There is a pause. Molly forces a smile

John Good! So — how was America, Sophie?
Sophie We were just telling Abby, we had a really good time …

The phone rings

Abby Excuse me. (*She answers the phone*)
Sophie The weather was great and the natives were friendly …
Raymond A bit too friendly sometimes …
Abby (*into the phone*) Hallo. … Darling — where are you? … Oh,
    splendid. … Well, we enjoyed your opening gambit. … Yes, we were
    getting quite cosy here in the candlelight. But your cryptic clue has
    defeated us so far. … They what? … Hang on a minute … (*To the
    others*) It's Léon on his mobile; he picked up Piers on the way, they're
    at the off-licence … (*Into the phone*) What's that? … They don't have
    what? … (*To John*) John, he says they don't have any Reserve; will
    Taylor's '85 do, whatever that is … ?

John grabs the phone

John (*into the phone*) Now listen, you old reprobate — only the very best
    will do, do you hear? … You can't palm me off with any old port in a storm,
    you know ——

*The others laugh. John makes as if to hand the phone back to Abby but
continues jokily*

    — and if you're not back here in double-quick time *you*'ll be the Winter
    of *my* discontent … (*He hands the phone back to Abby*)
Abby It's all right, darling. … Yes, the oven's fine — I'll turn it down …
    (*With a little extra emphasis*) Everything is on schedule — don't worry.
    (*She hangs up and looks at her watch*) Excuse me — a slave's work is never
    done … Do help yourselves to drinks …

Abby exits to the kitchen, closing the door

John So, what's the beef, kids? What's on the menu tonight?
Raymond Well, I'm sorry to disappoint you both but it's a meagre
    offering …

The music from the kitchen stops

John Oh, come on — we always gorge ourselves at these dos …

Raymond No, it's true — and when I say meagre I mean really meagre, more meagre than you can possibly imagine …

John What's he on about, Sophie? Has he been at the gin again?

Sophie Nothing to do with me …

John Léon always serves up a Bacchanalian feast, you know that …

Raymond Well, tonight, what will be served on your plate will be meagre — meagre baked in champagne with caviar cream sauce …

Abby enters and returns to the party, this time with her own drink. She attends to everybody during the following

Molly What on earth is that?

Sophie Don't worry, Moll, meagre is some kind of fish — sea bass, I think.

John Sea bass? You're sure it's not blowfish?

Raymond No, I don't think so … why?

John I wouldn't put it past our dear Léon to try that one. Eating blowfish is an ancient Japanese tradition. The only thing is … a single blowfish can contain enough poison to kill thirty people.

Abby (*to Sophie, stirring it*) Come to think of it, Léon did have a trip to Tokyo last year.

John Some varieties are quite harmless but others — well … Eating the liver is supposed to be good for male potency, but it can be the deadliest part. In Japan men take their wives out to dinner and order blowfish liver to impress them and prove their virility. Apparently it's considered equally macho for the chef to agree to cook it. Unfortunately several hundred Japanese die each year from eating them. Death comes slowly and agonizingly. First a tingling in the mouth, then numbness in the arms and legs and then laboured breathing and paralysis. It takes about five hours to die. It's a cruel death; you remain clear-headed to the end … Your brain is working but you know you're going to die.

Sophie How come you know so much about them?

Molly (*slightly tongue-in-cheek*) John is a collector of bizarre ways of killing people.

Raymond (*nervously*) No … Léon definitely said sea bass — didn't he, Abby? Sea bass …

Abby Yes, Ray — but don't forget the menu's supposed to be a secret. You're none of you to let on that you know.

John Well, sea bass it is, then. Sea bass with champagne and caviar — sounds devastating. Right … Well, the only way I'm going to kick the bucket tonight is through over-indulgence. Where's the Scotch?

During the following speech, we hear Léon's Range Rover arriving; headlights appear through the window

Raymond (*mainly to Molly, trying to cheer her up*) Hey, here's one for your collection, John. There was this item on the news on the local TV station in LA. Some guy who lives alone had always paid his rent by standing order through his bank. One day the standing order stopped, so the landlord asked the bank why. The bank said the account had run out of money. So — the landlord goes round to the apartment, opens the door and finds the guy dead in a chair with a five-year old TV guide on his lap. He had completely decomposed, the TV in the corner had burned out — but the Christmas fairy lights were still twinkling on and off.

We hear two car doors slam

Molly My, how gruesome …

The following offstage voices are muffled, barely distinguishable

Piers (*off; with a camp, Californian accent*) I'll take the port through the front way … (*In Léon's voice*) OK, thanks a lot, Piers …
Sophie My darling Ray, you do have the most extraordinary knack of saying the wrong thing at the wrong time.

The doorbell rings

I'll get it …

Sophie exits into the hall to answer the door

During the following, those onstage improvise a muffled conversation, John comparing notes with Raymond, etc.

Abby (*opening the kitchen door and calling through it*) Léon, the gang's all here … (*She moves away from the door, leaving it slightly ajar, then begins to top up drinks, hand round canapés, etc.*)

Abby and Molly chat, muffled, during the following

Piers (*off*) Sophie, darling, what a dress — you look good enough to eat. But that will have to come later. Be a doll, will you, and give this to Abby … I'm dying to go to the little boys' room. (*Calling out*) I'll be there in a whisper, everyone … !

Sophie enters with a bottle of port

Sophie Abby, Piers asked me to give you this. He won't be long, he's gone for a "tinkle". Oh, such a waste!

We hear a very loud gunshot coming from the direction of the kitchen. Everyone onstage turns in that direction

Abby (*softly*) Léon … Léon! (*She heads towards the kitchen*)

John restrains Abby

John Abby … No … Wait …
Piers (*off*) Hey … don't start the champagne without me …

We hear a second, very loud gunshot

Abby Léon!!!

Black-out

ACT II

SCENE 1

The same. Five days later. Daytime

When the CURTAIN *rises Chief Inspector Hubert Plum is discovered walking around the room slowly examining all and sundry. This takes some considerable time. Plum is an eccentric, provincial copper and a bit out of his depth with this case — or so everyone thinks. But beneath the slightly comic, bumbling exterior lies a sharp intellect. He must not be portrayed as a caricature but neither should his eccentricity be down-played. He carries a rumpled sheaf of papers in his hand. At some point he stops and stares at the audience, perhaps turning his head sideways or even upside down, to examine one or two of the rather weird pictures on display on the "fourth wall"*

Eventually we hear the front door open and voices in the hall; a Detective Sergeant is letting Raymond and Sophie into the house

Plum exits into the kitchen

Raymond and Sophie enter the room. There is a considerable pause before they speak

Raymond It's very strange coming back to this house.

Sophie I hope he has a very good reason for bringing us here.

Raymond You know, it's bizarre. We spend three weeks in Los Angeles, one of the most violent cities on earth, and nothing happens. Within two weeks of returning home we get this — in Banbury, of all places.

Sophie Poor John. This is all so terrible.

Raymond Oh yes ... Well — we all know where your sympathies lie. Or perhaps I should say "lay".

Sophie Ray, please — that was all over months ago.

Raymond Only because he ended it.

Sophie Ray, darling, I thought we'd made a pact.

Raymond So did I — but suddenly you're showing yourself in your true colours.

Sophie Whatever there was between John and me — is finished.

Raymond You know, if somebody did have it in for John last Friday, it could very well have been you. Revenge, they say, is sweet.

Sophie Jealousy, they say, is even sweeter.

Raymond Do you really think I'd kill a man over you? Over any woman, come to that.

Sophie Ray ... ! I'm trying to put all that behind us. It was just a flirtation — nothing happened.

Raymond Not for want of trying.

A pause

Anyway, it's not John you should feel sorry for — it's Léon. He's the one who's dead.

Sophie Yes, but whoever did it was after John, we know that now. And he's likely to try again.

Raymond And I suppose poor, innocent Léon doesn't matter a damn.

Sophie Yes, of course he does. But it's John we should be worried about now — he could still be in danger.

A pause

Raymond How was Abby today?

Sophie Jumpy ... Nervous as a kitten, to be precise. She kept asking if John was OK, was he being protected around the clock ...?

Plum enters backwards through the kitchen door, unbeknown to Raymond and Sophie

I must say she's hardly mentioned Léon all week; it's as if she's blotted his murder right out of her mind.

Raymond You can hardly blame her for that.

Sophie turns, sees Plum and is alarmed

Sophie Oh, my God!

Plum Forgive me, Mrs Brown, I didn't mean to startle you.

Raymond For heaven's sake, Inspector, we're jumpy enough as it is without you creeping up on us.

Plum Point taken, Mr Brown, point taken. I very much appreciate your coming here today ... I realize how distressing it must be for you — for you both. I've invited everyone who was here last Friday night to come along. Mrs Winter will be coming later; Mrs Drummond is with her at the moment. You see — I thought being here might jog your memories a little.

Raymond We've told you all we know, Inspector.

Plum Yes, I'm sure you have. I just wanted to ask you one more time, Mr Brown: when you arrived here that night — did you notice anything unusual? Do you remember any strangers outside the house, for instance?

Raymond No.

Plum Anything out of the ordinary in the street, in the driveway, in the garden ... ?

Raymond No.

Plum Mrs Brown?

Sophie No.

Plum Anything unusual — inside the house? Before the lights went out, that is.

Sophie You think he may have already been in this house — the killer?

Plum (*smiling at Sophie*) Mr Brown?

Raymond Everything was normal.

Plum Yes ... When you say "normal", what exactly do you mean?

Sophie I don't understand.

Raymond I mean — that we've been to many dinner parties at this house, Inspector, and they usually follow much the same routine. Last Friday was no exception. I'm not saying they were ever boring or anything, far from it, we always had a great time. It's just that the evening ... Well, it had a set pattern, that's all.

Plum Go on.

Raymond Well ... Sophie and I were invariably the first to get here; I'm a stickler for punctuality. Léon and me both; all those newspaper deadlines I have to meet, I suppose. We'd have a few drinks with Abby, the other guests would arrive, and then Léon would emerge with the fruits of his labour. Always ... Well, he really was a seriously good cook, Inspector — every time was a gastronomic experience.

Sophie He had a wonderful way with food ——

Raymond — and he was very generous with the wine — always the best. He was a great host, our Léon — full of bonhomie, full of laughs ...

Sophie He had a wicked sense of humour.

Raymond Yes, he loved practical jokes ... He had an almost childish obsession with them. Some were really evil.

Plum Tell me about them — please.

Sophie Inspector, shouldn't you be looking for the killer — whoever sent the threatening letters? Poor Léon was shot by mistake — we know that. I don't see what all this ——

Plum All in good time, Mrs Brown, all in good time. Mr Brown ... ?

Raymond Mm?

Plum You were about to acquaint me with Mr Winter's fondness for practical jokes ...

Raymond Was I? Well, with Léon it all started at school, according to Abby. He used to send his chums down to the hardware store for striped paint or a left-handed hammer or ... What was the other one? Oh yes, a pot of elbow grease — that was it. And it just carried on from there. Soon after we met Léon I had to cover a story in Warsaw for a couple of days, so he gave me this phrase to use; "A universal greeting in Polish", he said, "always use it when you meet someone for the first time — before you ask them directions, whatever". Well ... I was naïve and I fell for it. After twelve hours of funny looks I finally got it translated. It meant "Take off your knickers!" By then I'd said it to a policeman, a soldier in uniform and two nuns.

Sophie If ever foreign visitors asked Léon what they should do while they're in London he'd say, "My dear, you must try out the famous echo in the British Library Reading Room".

Raymond He used to get a real thrill going to Chinese restaurants that had fish tanks; mind you, they had to have goldfish in them. He used to carve a carrot into the shape of a fish and keep it in his pocket. Sometime during the meal he'd walk up to the fish tank with the carrot hidden in the palm of his hand, put his hand into the water, making sure everybody saw it, then take it out and pop the carrot into his mouth. He'd then crunch away merrily and eventually swallow it in full view of everybody. He was barred from at least two places that I know of, because of that.

Sophie Do you remember the time he borrowed a sign from the Salvation Army? It had "Jesus Saves" written across it. So he took it down the High Street, held it aloft and walked up and down outside one of the building societies.

Plum I see what you mean. Tell me, were dinner parties in this house invariably accompanied by practical jokes of some kind — the lights going out, the Hercule Poirot voice, that sort of thing?

Raymond No — hardly ever. Léon's extravaganzas were usually reserved for away matches — if you see what I mean.

Plum Did the Winters always invite the same guests?

Raymond No, no, far from it. We met all kinds of people here.

Sophie (*sarcastically*) Librarians, undertakers ...

Raymond Molly and John were frequently here and, of course — we weren't *always* invited.

Plum (*referring to his papers*) In your statement you said that when you arrived Mr Winter was about to leave — on his way to the off-licence.

Sophie That's right — they'd forgotten the port for John. He usually consumed the lion's share of a bottle of Dow's every time he came.

Plum And how long was Mr Winter gone?

Raymond We've already told you this, Inspector.

Plum Just tell me one more time, Mr Brown.

Raymond About half an hour, I'd say, maybe less.

Plum I believe there was music playing in the kitchen?

Raymond Yes, Léon always played music while he cooked. They were his twin passions: the classics and food.

Plum So he was listening to the radio.

Raymond More likely CDs, tapes, whatever — he had quite a collection. Sometimes it was like the Royal Albert Hall in that kitchen — you couldn't hear yourself think.

Plum And this music continued to play while Mr Winter was out of the house?

Sophie Er ... Yes, yes ... It did.

Plum Right up till the moment he returned?

Raymond I believe so, yes. Apart from during the power cut, of course.

Sophie Are you saying you think the killer hid in the kitchen while Léon was out of the house? With the three of us in here — talking?

Plum It's possible, Mrs Brown.

Sophie Oh, Ray, what a ghastly thought.

Raymond And we didn't hear him because the music was still playing ...

Sophie (*horrified*) He must have been in the house while I was sitting here in the dark.

Plum So ... Apart from the black-out and the mystery voice there was nothing about that night that was any different from any other dinner party night in this house?

Raymond Not really.

Sophie Only the burnt toast.

Plum Yes ... Sorry ... ?

Sophie I smelt burning and thought Léon had blotted his copybook. It turned out Abby had burnt the melba toast.

Plum Hm. Nothing else?

Sophie Not as I recall.

We hear the front door open and the voices of John and the Detective Sergeant

Plum (*to Raymond and Sophie*) I may ask you that question again before we finish here; when I've had a chance to jog your memories.

John enters

(*To John*) Mr Drummond, thank you for coming so promptly.

John I didn't have much choice — your coppers were shadowing me all the way. Ray — Sophie. Look ... I really have told you everything I know, Inspector. I've been over it several times with your sergeant down at the nick.

Plum Yes, I know, but now I'd like you to go over it again with me, if you don't mind. It's just possible, you see, you may have overlooked something — inadvertently, of course. If you were the intended target last Friday evening then they could try again. The sooner we catch them the better.

Sophie Them?

Plum There may be more than one person involved. (*He refers again to his papers*) Now, Mr Drummond, tell me, if you would, about these threatening letters you received. According to your statement, you believe them to be from a business partner of yours?

John He's not a partner — just somebody I do business with.

Plum How long have you known him?

John About a year. I've had three deals with him in the last nine months.

Plum What sort of deals?

John Import ... export. It's what I do .The first two were no problem — very profitable for both of us. But this last one ...

Plum He's South African, you say?

John Yes, but he operates out of Zimbabwe. Look, do you mind if I help myself to a drink? I've been on the road all day. I'm sure Abby won't mind.

Plum I don't see why not.

John Thank you. (*He pours himself a drink during the following*) On the face of it, it was a good deal: a consignment of copper, top quality stuff. It wasn't substandard in any way ... I've still got it in my warehouse — you can have it tested if you like.

Plum Nobody's suggesting that, Mr Drummond. So what went wrong?

John After I'd bought it the bottom fell out of the market; the copper market has a habit of doing that, I'm afraid.

Raymond Oh yes, I remember.

John Vansittart started to get nervous — that's his name, the South African. Not that there was anything illegal going on; the stuff wasn't stolen, or anything like that, it's just that — well — I couldn't sell the stuff for love nor money ... I couldn't give it away.

Plum So you weren't able to pay your man in Zimbabwe — this Mr ... er ...

John Vansittart ... no ...

Plum Didn't you have any cash in reserve?

John No. All my profits were tied up in other deals ... That's the way I operate — I always look for a quick turnover.

Plum Isn't that rather risky?

John Yes. As I now know to my cost. I couldn't pay him because I didn't have a bean.

Plum How many times did you meet this man?

John I never met him — it was all done by email and fax and intermediaries. He's a bit of a mysterious character, I'm afraid.

Plum And then you received the threatening letters?
John Two of them — one a week after the other.

Plum shuffles his collection of papers and extracts photocopies of the two threatening letters, the originals of which were made up of newspaper cuttings stuck on to a blank sheet of paper

Plum (*referring to the first photocopy*) "If you do not pay me — what you owe me — then your life — will not be worth living." (*He passes the first photocopy to Raymond and then refers to the second*) "We had a contract — which you have dishonoured. I have now taken out another contract — which can only be honoured — by your death." (*He passes this copy round*) How do you know these letters were from — er — this South African chappie?
John Well, who else would have sent them? I don't get death threats every day, you know.
Raymond I've been in the newspaper business for twenty years; I come across this kind of threat all the time. This is the first time I've ever known anyone try to carry it out.
Plum Yes, quite. They were posted by hand at your home …
John Yes …
Plum No postmark or postage …
John (*wearily*) Naturally …
Plum And yet — rather a strange method to use, wouldn't you say? Cutting out words from a newspaper and sticking them on a sheet of paper … I mean, it's so theatrical — like something out of a Hollywood film. (*He pronounces it "filum"*)
John It's probably the only way he could be sure of spelling it right.
Plum (*thinking this is an intelligent suggestion*) Oh, yes — well done … Yes, as you told my sergeant, the South African chappie's English — was very poor …
John Practically non-existent; he's Afrikaans. That's why we did business through intermediaries.
Plum And yet the English grammar in both anonymous letters was impeccable. He must have got somebody else to do it for him — wouldn't you say? (*He gathers in the two letters*)

A pause

Why didn't you tell the police about these threats, Mr Drummond?
John Well … When I got the first letter I didn't really take it seriously.
Plum And when you received the second letter?
John All right, I did take it seriously then. I just didn't think phoning the police would do any good, that's all.

Plum Well ... thank you for your confidence. Who else saw them? Besides yourself, I mean?

John Only Molly. I was trying to hide them from her but ... I couldn't help it ... she was there when I opened the second letter.

Plum Ah, yes. Did you show them to Mr Winter, by any chance?

John Léon? No.

Plum You're certain of that?

John Of course. I told him what was in the letters but he never saw them ... the letters never left my house until your Sergeant came to collect them.

Plum I see.

A pause. He refers once more to his papers

Plum You and Mr Winter were very close, I believe, Mr Drummond? Would that be right?

John Yes, we were close ... We had a lot in common ... We had no secrets from each other ...

Plum (*referring to another document*) Is that why you drove identical cars?

John The Range Rovers? I suppose so ...

Plum And the number plates (*another document*) P - one - N - K - Y and P - E - R - K - one.

John Pinky and Perky ... Yes ... It was one of his jokes ...

Plum Another one of his jokes ... Yes, I see. Now, Mr Drummond ... (*referring to another document; slowly and deliberately*) according to your statement here, last Friday evening you drove to a dinner party at this house in your wife's car because your own car, a dark green Range Rover, had a puncture. And when Léon Winter arrived back from the off-licence in his own, identical dark green Range Rover — you are suggesting that a killer, hired by your South African chappie, mistook Mr Winter for yourself and killed him ...

John (*emphatically*) Yes ...

Plum Except there was no puncture, was there?

John Inspector ...

Plum There was no puncture on your car — was there, Mr Drummond?

John Well, no — not exactly.

Plum Last Friday night when I sent my officers round to your house to check your story, they found your Range Rover with four fully inflated tyres and no evidence of any puncture whatsoever.

John But I thought there was. (*With the weariness of one who has said this many times before*) Look — there was a huge gash on the side of the tyre and it was flat on the ground. When your Sergeant came back and told me he'd found nothing ... Well — at first, I couldn't believe it. But then Ray, thank God, came to my rescue ...

Raymond It was Léon — had to be; he faked the whole thing.

Plum Isn't that just a little far-fetched?

John Not if you'd known Léon Winter it isn't. Think about it, Inspector — all he has to do is stick some kind of rubber solution on the side of the tyre, make a gash in it to look as if someone had vandalized the tyre, then let the air out …

Plum (*amusedly*) I hardly think ——

Raymond And knowing that John would then abandon the Range Rover and come round here in Molly's car, Léon nips back as soon as they've left, removes the rubber solution and pumps up the tyre. It's as if John imagined the whole thing. The trip to the off-licence was bogus, Inspector — Léon never ran out of port or anything else. He was too well-organized. It was just an excuse to return to John and Molly's house.

John That slashed tyre looked totally real …

Raymond It may have looked real, but I know Léon. Look, he's tried it before. Darling, do you remember that dinner at Felicity's? There was a knock on the front door, right? When Felicity opened it Léon was there, alone. He collapsed on the hall carpet with a four-inch stab wound under his heart and covered in blood. He then proceeded to give a five-minute dying speech on the floor in front of eight dinner guests. We twigged what was going on but the others didn't. The stab wound — was rubber solution — and pints of stage blood. The real icing on the cake was that one of the guests was a doctor — and Léon knew that! He was really testing them to the limit that night.

Plum But why would he fake the puncture?

Raymond He was up to his old tricks again … there doesn't have to be a reason.

Plum If what you say is true, then we seem to be inundated with … well, I'm not sure … what do you suppose *is* the collective noun for practical jokes?

Raymond But he meant no harm, Inspector. He just wanted to make people laugh. There was no malice in Léon.

Plum So you're trying to tell me that Léon Winter set up a phoney puncture that went horribly wrong, and, by some quirk of fate, resulted in his own death?

Raymond That's what it looks like.

John This has Léon's signature written all over it. Ray saw it coming a mile off. He should know — he's been the butt of Léon's endless pranks for years.

Sophie (*wearily*) That's very true, Inspector, I'm afraid to say.

Plum (*finding another document*) But according to Mr Piers Gerard's statement, he met Mr Winter at the traffic lights down the road and Mr Winter invited him to accompany him to the off-licence. At no time did Mr Winter have any opportunity to return to your house and remove the evidence of his so-called "puncture". So who did remove it, Mr Drummond?

John I don't know.
Plum Neither do I ...

A pause

Mr Brown?
Raymond Pass.
Plum Mm!

A pause

Now ... This South African chappie (*he consults his papers*) Mr ... er ...
(*he reads the name and his pronunciation is something akin to "Vancy
tart"*) Mr Vansittart ... Ha — well — never trust a man with a name like
that! Can you think of anyone else, Mr Drummond, apart from him, who
may have wished you harm?
John How do you mean?
Plum Someone else you'd done business with, perhaps ...
John No, of course not. There are umpteen people I may have got the better
of in a business deal. They may have resented it — but not to the point of
killing me ...
Plum What about your friends; anyone in your social circle?
John My dear Inspector, if I knew of anyone who wanted me dead they
wouldn't still be my friend, now would they ... ?
Plum Unless it was a friend who turned out to be anything but ...
Sophie What is that supposed to mean?
Plum Mr Drummond — your two anonymous letters were naturally
examined by our forensic department; fingerprints were found and after
eliminating your own and your wife's we were left with a third set of prints
— on the second letter only. Now — are you quite positive that nobody else
handled that second letter?
John Absolutely ...
Plum So the third set of prints must have been already there — maybe
belonging to Mr Vansittart (*it has now become "Fancy tart"*) himself.
John Can you trace them?
Plum We ran them through the police computer — but found nothing.
Clearly Mr Vansittart (*"Fancy tart"*) has no criminal record.
John Damn!
Plum But then we had a stroke of luck. Following normal procedure,
forensics ran a fingerprint check on the murder scene — and naturally we
compared the prints of your letter with those we found in there ... (*He
indicates the kitchen*)
Sophie You mean to establish if Vansittart had been in the kitchen that night?

Plum Precisely …

John And?

Plum He had. We found a match …

John Well, that's great. It proves that Vansittart was the killer.

Plum Not quite, Mr Drummond. Not so much the killer as the victim; the prints on the threatening letter matched those of your poor, deceased friend. You see — Léon Winter and Mr Vansittart (*"Fancy tart"*) would appear to be one and the same man.

Raymond Is this some kind of joke, Inspector?

Plum If it is, it's certainly not one of mine. But it may very well be one of Léon Winter's.

John But that's impossible — Léon would never …

John and Raymond look at each other

Raymond Oh yes, he would …

Plum If Mr Winter was responsible for the threatening letters then I suppose it is just possible he was responsible for the fake puncture also. But whatever he had in mind — somehow I don't think his own death was the intended outcome.

We hear the front door open and the voices of Abby, Molly and the Detective Sergeant

Abby and Molly enter. Abby is clutching a book

Sophie Abby! Come and sit here.

Molly She's still suffering from shock.

Sophie Inspector, I really don't think it was a good idea to bring her here today.

Plum Point taken, Mrs Brown, point taken.

Abby It's all right, Sophie. I want Léon's killer caught and put behind bars — and if this is what it takes, then so be it.

Plum Thank you, Mrs Winter. I shall try not to keep you any longer than is necessary. Please sit down, Mrs Drummond. That seems to be everyone apart from Mr Gerard; apparently he's attending an antiques fair in Cheltenham. He said he'd join us as soon as he could. (*He looks at his watch*) Now — cast your minds back, if you would, to last Friday evening. We know the black-out that occurred here that night was engineered by a timing device attached to the electricity supply. A similar device was found with a battery-operated tape recorder that fed the Hercule Poirot voice to the speaker system. Léon Winter's fingerprints were found on both devices and also on the cryptic note found taped to the fuse-box. All this appears to be part of an intricate practical joke that Mr Winter had planned for the benefit of you — his guests.

John Léon admitted as much on the phone to Abby.

Plum Yes, quite. Were you aware, Mrs Winter, that any of this was going to happen?

Abby No — not at all. I was as much in the dark as anyone else.

Plum Yes, of course, thank you. I have a copy of the note here. (*He produces it*) "Now is the winter…". Winter is, of course, his own name, we know that — but it could also be a quotation from ——

Sophie Shakespeare … Yes, I think we all know that, Inspector — the opening line from *Richard III*.

Plum (*crestfallen at having been pre-empted*) Yes, it would appear so … "Now is the winter — of our discontent …"

John What the hell does that mean?

Raymond I've no idea, but I'm sure the inspector is about to enlighten us.

Plum Well — you flatter me. I was rather hoping that one of *you* might be able to enlighten *me*. (*A pause*) No … ? No! Oh well … that will have to wait a while, I'm afraid. Now, as to the actual murder itself, I was rather hoping that bringing you all here today might jog your collective memory. You see, I'm afraid the evidence we have gathered so far poses more questions than it provides answers. Firstly, there are the bullets that killed your husband, Mrs Winter. They had quite deep scratch marks on them … It could have been a very old and well-worn weapon — or they could have been caused by a silencer …

Sophie Well, that's ridiculous, we all heard the shots loud and clear — it's a wonder no-one dropped dead from the shock … (*She realizes, too late, that was an unfortunate remark to make*)

Plum Yes, of course — must have been an old gun; a war souvenir, perhaps. Once we find the weapon we'll know for sure.

Abby You haven't found it yet?

Plum No, we haven't. We've searched the immediate area, but so far, no sign. Secondly — there are the fingerprints found in the kitchen. Now this is one area where we have made a little progress, isn't that so, Mr Drummond? None but your own prints, Mrs Winter, and your husband's. (*He gives a meaningful look to the others*) Not even your cleaning lady's, Mrs —— ?

Abby Josie …

Plum Mrs Thomas, yes. Odd, wouldn't you think? That she didn't leave any fingerprints in the kitchen?

Abby She always wore gloves when she was cleaning …

Plum (*somewhat disappointed*) Ah … Yes … That would explain it. Tell me — did she clean the rest of the house as well? Or just the kitchen? (*He wanders around the room during the following*)

Abby Well, not every week, no — but over a period of time she would have, yes.

Sophie Inspector, what on earth has this got to do with Josie? She was at home with her husband that night, you know that …

Plum Yes, of course — I must crave your indulgence; it's just that her fingerprints can be found in some of the other rooms in the house but none in the kitchen — not one.

Sophie Why were you fingerprinting the other rooms in the house? Léon was murdered in there! (*She points to the kitchen*)

Plum (*pointedly*) Oh, we're very thorough, Mrs Brown, very thorough.

Abby So is Josie …

Plum Yes, so it would seem …

The telephone rings

   Plum exits into the kitchen

Raymond Shall I get that, Abby?

Abby nods. Raymond answers the phone

   (*Into the phone*) Hallo, Mrs Winter's house. … Who? … Yes, he is. Just a moment.

   Plum enters, closing the kitchen door

It's for you, Inspector.

Plum For me? Oh, thank you. Excuse me. (*He takes the phone; into it*) Hallo. (*He utters a deep sigh*) Muriel, you know better than to ring me here. How did you get the number, anyhow? … Oh, I see. … Did I? … I did? … Oh dear, how very remiss of me. … Yes, I'll send a car for it straight away. Yes. … Thank you, dear. … Goodbye. (*He hangs up*) Excuse me, er, Mrs Winter — that was my wife … I shan't be long.

   Plum exits into the hallway

There is a pause

Abby I've been reading this book that Molly found for me. It's a biography of Alphonse Allais, French artist and illusionist. That's one of his paintings up there (*she refers to the totally black canvas on the wall*) — he called it "Black Men Fighting In A Cave At Night". He painted another canvas completely red and called it (*she refers to the book*) — "Apoplectic

Cardinals Harvesting Tomatoes By The Red Sea" and then a totally white one — "Anaemic Young Girls Going To Their First Communion Through A Blizzard". Léon would have loved it … Bless you, Molly.
Molly It was nothing.

A pause

Abby I shall miss him, you know.
John We shall all miss him, Abby.
Sophie All of us.
Raymond I'll miss his cooking.

Sophie digs Raymond in the ribs

Raymond Well, him too … I mean — I'll miss — him …

A pause

John April Fools' Day will never be the same without him.
Raymond Years ago, when I was a cub reporter on Capital Radio, they announced on air on April first that to compensate for the forty-eight hours that had been lost since the war because of switching between Greenwich Mean Time and British Summer Time, the fifth and twelfth of April for that year were to be cancelled. One chap rang in and asked if he'd have to pay his staff for those two days, another said his house sale was to be completed on the fifth — would it still be valid? And several rang in with birthdays on those dates: would they still be a year older? I often think Léon must have been on the news desk that day.

Abby smiles

Plum returns carrying yet more pieces of paper

Plum I do apologize — it seems I left an important document on the kitchen table this morning. I've sent one of my officers round to retrieve it. Now — where was I before I was so rudely interrupted?
Raymond Fingerprints.
Plum I beg your pardon? Oh yes, yes — of course. Your husband's fingerprints appear to be cropping up everywhere, Mrs Winter. You see, they were also found on the second threatening letter sent to Mr Drummond here. It's just possible that these letters together with the phantom puncture were yet more elements of your husband's elaborate charade.
John I'm afraid it appears to be true, Abby. Though what Léon was up to I really have no idea.

Plum If your husband did indeed send the letters then he appears to have been masquerading as a businessman from Zimbabwe named Vansittart (*"fancy tart"*). Were you aware of any of this, Mrs Winter?

Abby Certainly not.

Plum Does the name Vansittart (*"fancy tart"*) mean anything to you?

John (*correcting him*) Van*sit*tart!

Plum Whatever ... Does it?

The name obviously means something to Abby, but she hides her knowledge from Plum

Abby No.

Plum Thank you — that tells me a great deal. Now it occurred to me that this false identity of your husband's, if it was indeed such, may have extended further. So I took it upon myself to fax his fingerprints to Zimbabwe via Johannesburg. Zimbabwe drew a blank, but the South African police put them through their computer and came up with a match — quite by chance! An amazing stroke of luck, really. You see, it appears that about ten years ago a young couple living in South Africa were burgled and the police had taken their fingerprints to eliminate them from the prints found around their home, much as we've done here — all standard procedure, of course. Now it is also standard procedure to destroy such prints at the end of an investigation in order that no innocent person's fingerprints are ever kept on file. We do the same in this country. (*He smiles*) I see you are ahead of me — yes, the South African police had neglected to destroy them; very remiss of them — but most fortunate for me. And the young man's prints, which had remained on file for the last ten years, matched those of Léon Winter. But his name then was Noël Sumner — S, U, M for Muriel, N — for Norbert, E, R. Léon is the reverse of Noël. Winter is the reverse of — well, Sumner, Summer, close enough. Obviously the same man. I then took the liberty of faxing Mrs Winter's prints, taken from the kitchen here, to Johannesburg and — lo and behold — another match! Mrs Abby Winter turns out to be Mrs Gloria Sumner ... Isn't that extraordinary? Apparently she worked as a publishing editor in South Africa and her maiden name was VAN*SIT*TART! (*He pronounces Vansittart correctly for the first time*)

Black-out

SCENE 2

The action is continuous

The Lights come up

Plum Isn't that your real name, Mrs Winter — Gloria Sumner?
Abby Yes.
Plum And your maiden name was Vansittart?
Abby Yes.
Plum But when I asked you if the name meant anything to you, you said no.
Abby It's a common enough name in South Africa, I just didn't think. Besides, your pronunciation was a little awry. Look, I have done nothing wrong, Inspector. Léon and I simply decided on a complete change of identity when we began our new life here in England. I have committed no crime — neither had Léon. I think you'll find that neither of us has a criminal record anywhere in the world.
Plum You may never have been convicted of a crime but that does not mean that you have never committed one.
John Now just a minute ——
Plum As far as the South African police were concerned the trail stopped there — but I asked them to dig a little deeper and they quickly discovered that Mr Noël Sumner had supposedly "died" … (*he looks at another paper*) in a boating accident on Lake Tanganyika five years ago. His wife, Gloria, received payment from a life insurance policy totalling some three million Rand. Soon afterwards she left the country.
Abby So now he's really dead. Rather ironic, isn't it?
Plum But this time I think you killed him, Mrs Winter.

Abby smiles at the absurdity of this suggestion

All (*variously*) Oh now, Inspector … That's absurd … How dare you suggest …
Raymond Inspector, is this your idea of old-fashioned detective work, scattering accusations around like confetti? I've never heard anything so ridiculous.
Plum Yes, it is rather banal, isn't it? But just humour me a while longer, Mr Brown. Let us examine Léon Winter's cryptic clue a little more closely. "Now is the winter of our discontent." The only remaining "winter" is his wife … "Our discontent" would certainly appear to be his own death. So, can anyone continue the quotation?
Sophie "Now is the winter of our discontent, made — glorious — summer — by …"
Plum Exactly … "made glorious summer" … Or, given a slightly different reading, "now is the winter of our discontent made 'Gloria … Sumner'". You husband would appear to be suggesting that you were somehow implicated in his death, Mrs Sumner.
John Now, look here ——
Abby (*very sure of herself*) I hardly think that's what he meant, Inspector.

I was standing right there when my husband was shot and I have witnesses to prove it.

All That's right, Inspector — we were all here ...

Plum Yes, of course — of course ...

Abby Five witnesses, to be exact.

The Sergeant ushers in Piers, who is now in full flow with his camp, Californian persona

Plum Four, Mrs Sumner. Mr Gerard was in the — "little boys' room".

Piers Do I detect my ears burning? Well — there's enough policemen out there to start a riot. Oh, sorry. I didn't know there was a gathering. Sorry, Abby.

Abby That's OK, Piers.

Plum Thank you for coming, Mr Gerard.

Piers I came as soon as I could, but there's so much traffic ...

Plum That's quite all right.

Piers (*joining Abby on the sofa*) Are you OK, Abby?

Abby I'm fine, thank you Piers.

Piers It may seem like you're going through hell at the moment, but it will pass, believe me. (*With meaning*) Paradise — has not been lost — forever.

Abby You're very sweet, Piers.

Plum Now that Mr Gerard has been able to join us, we can move the investigation a stage further. You were, of course, the last person to see Mr Winter alive, Mr Gerard — after your return from the off-licence ...

Piers If you mean the liquor store, yes. How could I ever forget. If I'd come in the back way instead of the front it might have been me that was killed and not Léon ...

Plum Tell me again — exactly where you bumped into each other.

Piers At the traffic lights on the corner. I was on my way to the dinner party, of course, so I asked him where he was going and he said, "My soufflé failed to rise, so I'm off to the Chinese take-away!" Typical Léon. So I hopped in and we went to the liquor store.

Plum Good — good! I would now like to establish who was the last person to see Mr Winter alive — before he left this house.

Raymond Well, that was myself, my wife and Abby ...

Plum Did you see Mr Winter before he left, Mrs Brown?

Sophie Yes, he was still here when we arrived. His car was still outside.

Plum But did you actually see him?

Sophie No, I suppose I didn't.

Plum Or you, Mr Brown?

Raymond Yes, of course ... Well, I may not have actually seen him but I certainly heard him. He was chopping something at one point and I heard the food mixer going ... I spoke to him through the door — and we both saw his car through the window as he left ...

Sophie And we heard him talking to Abby. She's the only one allowed in the kitchen when he's cooking … He's very secretive — was — very secretive …

Plum So — Mrs Winter — was the only person to actually *see* her husband before he left the house …

Raymond I guess so, yes.

Plum And Mr Gerard — was the only person to see him when he came back to the house …

Abby Where is all this leading, Inspector?

Plum I've no idea, Mrs Winter. But I'm very much hoping it will lead somewhere. Now — moving on; after the first shot, what exactly happened then?

Raymond Well … Abby called Léon's name and then started toward the kitchen door — but John stopped her …

John I grabbed her about here (*he moves to the spot*) and said something like "Abby … no … wait." Then we heard the second shot and Abby screamed "Léon!". Then I ran towards the door.

Plum Show me, would you, Mr Drummond?

John (*taking up a position by the kitchen doorway*) I was about here — with Abby behind me. When I reached the door I waited a moment then opened it …

Plum encourages him to do so

(*Opening the door and looking in*) As I entered the kitchen I looked to the left … There was no-one there but — er — I could see the back door was open. When I looked to the right I saw Léon slumped on the floor by the Aga.

Piers (*raising his hand like a schoolboy*) It was about then that I came into this room —

Plum And then?

The Sergeant enters carrying a document

John I ran to him … I put my arm on his shoulder, and as he rolled on to his back I could see the bullet holes in his chest.

The Sergeant hands the document to Plum and stays in the room

Plum Go on.

John I felt the pulse in his neck, but he was dead. One of his eyes was half open. But there was hardly any blood.

Plum Hm. You say he rolled on to his back … How was he lying when you first approached?

John On his side.

Plum Which side?

John His right-hand side facing the Aga.

Plum You're sure of that?

John Absolutely.

Plum Now, this is important, Mr Drummond: how much time had elapsed between you hearing the shots and the moment you touched his shoulder and he rolled on to his back?

John Well — no more than a minute, I suppose.

Plum There you have it — no more than a minute! Thank you, Mr Drummond, I think we now have all the answers! (*He holds up the document handed to him by the Sergeant*) This is the document I left on my breakfast table this morning; it is the pathologist's report, including the results of the post-mortem on Léon Winter's body. It contains one item that didn't seem to fit the known facts, it's been troubling me all day. You see, I hadn't taken note of — the pattern of lividity.

Molly The pattern of what ... ?

Plum The pattern of lividity, Mrs Drummond. You see, it is virtually impossible for science to pinpoint accurately the time of death, any death. I'm afraid television pathologists have powers not granted to ordinary mortals. But what we can tell with some certainty is the position of the body — at the time of death. You see, when the heart stops beating the blood drains to the lowest part of the body. This is called the pattern of lividity. If a victim dies face down and is later propped up in a standing position, the lividity would be concentrated in the front of the body rather than in the feet. Similarly, if someone had died hanging upside down and was later laid upon the ground, the lividity would remain in the head. This pattern of lividity is usually completed between thirty minutes and two hours after death. (*Referring to the document*) Now, the pathologist's report states, firstly, that Léon Winter died instantly from his wounds. This explains the lack of blood — it would have remained within his chest cavity. Secondly it states that the lividity in his body was already concentrated down his right-hand side.

John Yes, that's how I found him — lying on his right-hand side.

Plum But you said he lay like that for less than a minute after you heard the shots before rolling on his back. Therefore, if the pattern of lividity was already concentrated down his right-hand side, then he must have already lain dead in that position — for at least thirty minutes — probably more.

John But I would have known; he would have been cold.

Plum Not necessarily. The rate at which dead bodies cool varies enormously; the surrounding air temperature can be a determining factor and Mr Winter's body lay in the warmest part of the kitchen next to the Aga cooker. I once examined a corpse which had lain dead in a body-bag for three hours; it was just as warm to the touch as a live person.

John But he would have been stiff by then. When he rolled over, his arm just flopped to the floor.

Plum Not so, I'm afraid. Rigor mortis does not set in immediately. In any case it starts in the smaller muscles, like those of the jaw and hands, and usually proceeds to the larger ones, such as in the arm, over the course of six to twelve hours.

Raymond I'm afraid you've lost me, Inspector.

Molly What does all this mean?

Plum Allow me to explain.

Piers Please do.

Plum First of all: I believe the impersonation of Vansittart, the fake puncture, the black-out, the Hercule Poirot voice, were all part of a labyrinthine practical joke set up by Léon Winter — the purpose of which we may never know. Its effect on my enquiries, however, was that of a glorious "red herring" ...

Sophie Baked in caviar cream sauce, no doubt ...

Plum I'm sorry ... ?

Sophie Nothing, Inspector ...

Plum Mm! But I'm inclined to believe Mr Winter's motive was mischief rather than malice ... If a crime had been intended he would hardly have left his fingerprints for the police to find. I also believe Mrs Winter may have been a party to, at least, some of this masquerade — but at some stage she decided to hijack her husband's plan for her own ends. As for last Friday night, it is my contention that, when Mr and Mrs Brown arrived, Léon Winter — was already dead ——

There is a reaction from the others

— lying on his side by the Aga in the kitchen. As for the smell of burnt toast, Mrs Brown, I suspect that may well have been the remains of cordite — left by the gun which had already killed him. It is also my belief that Mr Winter's voice in conversation with his wife in the kitchen — together with the chopping noises and other associated cooking sounds — were provided by: Mr Piers Gerard. As a former professional actor, it would not be difficult for him to disguise his voice through a half-open doorway with music playing.

Molly But the shots, Inspector, we all heard the shots, and Abby was in here.

Piers And I was powdering my nose, so get your laughing gear round that one, Mr "Clever Detective".

Plum I shall try, Mr Gerard, I shall try.

During this sequence, Plum acts out his version of events, using the curtains, the phone, etc.

Plum Once the Browns had arrived it was, of course, Mr Gerard who left in the Range Rover and called at the off-licence — alone. The manager's description confirms that. I believe, in your statement, Mr Gerard, you claimed that you'd left Mr Winter in the car — "with the engine running." Hm! A nice touch, that, a nice touch. Having left the off-licence Mr Gerard then returned to a position, perhaps somewhere in the side street opposite, where he could clearly see the driveway to this house. From there he would have witnessed the black-out, which, of course, came as a complete surprise to everybody having been engineered by Léon Winter alone. Once the Drummonds had arrived, Mr Gerard was no doubt highly relieved to see the power restored. He then telephoned this number on Léon Winter's mobile phone — pretending to be him. Mrs Winter answered, of course. (*He picks up the phone*) But I believe you actually spoke to him too, Mr Drummond — though, luckily for Mr Gerard, it was not necessary for him to reply. Now the next sequence had to be very carefully timed. At a pre-arranged signal — probably the end of the phone call (*he replaces the phone*) — Mrs Winter closed these curtains to mask what was about to happen in the driveway outside. She then turned off the music in the kitchen, removed the music tape, inserted a new tape, switched it on and returned to this room. This second tape would have contained a precisely timed period of silence followed by two gunshots. An idea Mrs Winter may well have copied from one of her husband's hare-brained schemes. Mr Gerard, meanwhile, at the same pre-arranged signal would have known precisely how much time he had to fill as he crossed the road, entered the drive, parked the Range Rover, returned Mr Winter's hat and coat to the kitchen, held a muffled conversation with *himself* in the driveway outside, continued round to the front door, rang the doorbell, entered the hall and retired to the "little boys' room" — moments before the first gunshot was heard. After the second gunshot the tape would have continued in silence while Mr Drummond entered the kitchen and found Mr Winter's body still lying on its side by the Aga, where it had lain for the past hour or so, its pattern of lividity by now firmly established.

Piers Inspector, you really should join our amateur dramatics troupe; you're very convincing.

Plum (*referring once more to his notes*) Mr Gerard, can you confirm that prior to your moving to this area five months ago you worked as the Events Manager at the Guilfoyle Hotel in Ambleside in the Lake District?

Piers How did you know that … ?

Plum Oh, it was quite easy — a little old-fashioned detective work, nothing more. Is that correct, Mr Gerard?

Piers Yes …

Plum And can you confirm, Mrs Winter, that about six months ago you stayed at the same hotel while attending a book fair?

Sophie You are a mine of information.

Plum We're very thorough, Mrs Brown, very thorough. And can you both verify that during that period you enjoyed an intimate relationship together?

Piers We became friends, but that's all …

Plum You became lovers, Mr Gerard …

Piers I'm afraid I don't play that side of the fence, Inspector …

Plum Several members of staff are prepared to substantiate that.

Piers They always were a nosey bunch — Peeping Toms the lot of 'em …

Plum How do you explain that, Mr Gerard?

Piers Sometimes I like to see how the other half loves …

Abby That'll do, Piers …

By now the others are pretty dumbstruck

Sophie (*to Abby*) I thought you didn't meet him till long after he moved here.

Plum When Mr Gerard moved to this area he took his time befriending the Winters so as not to arouse suspicion. Or perhaps I should call you Mr York. I have got your full name correctly, haven't I, sir? It is Piers Gerard York? Is it not?

Piers (*tentatively*) Yes — that's right …

Plum Well, now, that would seem to complete our quotation from *Richard III*: "Now is the winter — of our discontent — made Gloria Sumner — by this son of York".

Piers What is he talking about?

Plum Shakespeare, Mr York. The Immortal Bard. A frequent visitor to Banbury in his day. Mr Winter would appear to be implicating both of you in his untimely death.

Piers What? (*He looks to the others*)

The others stare at Piers in horror

Well, there's no need to look at me like that — I may be a friend of Dorothy but it doesn't mean to say I'm a bad person! (*He looks at Abby and shrugs*) All right, Rod Steiger may have said it first but I'm not proud.

Abby You have a fertile imagination, Inspector.

Plum I think not, Mrs Winter. Mr York's only opportunity to dispose of the gun was on his trip to the off-licence — not a great distance, we'll find it eventually — and the silencer, too, I shouldn't wonder. As for your silent tape with the gunshots … Well, we sealed off the kitchen the night of the murder; it could very well be amongst the myriad of tapes we removed from there this morning — we'll find that eventually, too. By the way, the pathologist's report also contains the results of tests made on a pair of yellow rubber gloves found in the kitchen … They make very interesting reading. Now, if you would both care to leave by the front door, my Sergeant will accompany you.

Piers (*back to his normal, English, masculine self*) No more weekends in Stroud, Abby. Paradise is postponed.

Piers exits

Abby (*rising and moving to Plum*) If you hadn't chanced on our fingerprints in South Africa, you would never have put this together, would you?

Plum Never say never, Mrs Winter! I must confess the South African police deliberately retained your fingerprints — they were highly suspicious of the both of you.

Abby turns and tosses the book on to the sofa. She heads for the exit

Abby (*referring to the book*) Nice try, Molly.

Abby exits

Plum (*to the others*) Well ... Thank you for your patience. I need detain you no longer.

Sophie Inspector, do you mean to say that this whole, camp persona of Piers' was a pretence?

Plum As false as the Californian accent, I'm afraid. He adopted both to throw you off the scent when he moved here to continue his affair with Mrs Winter.

Sophie Oh, what a waste!

Plum A complete fabrication, I'm afraid. Apart from the fact that he was, at one time, a professional actor.

John But the puncture that never was ... ?

Plum Mr Brown's suspicions were quite correct: all part of Mr Winter's entertainment for the evening. What else he had in store for you I have no idea. It's just possible there are other surprises lying around this house still waiting to happen. The next occupants may well be in for a housewarming they hadn't bargained for. Ha — wicked!

John Yes, but who removed the rubber solution and re-inflated the tyre if Léon was already dead?

Plum Piers Gerard again, I'm afraid. When he left here for the off-licence he was, of course, alone and had plenty of time to return to your house. He needed to remove the phantom puncture to throw suspicion on to you.

Moll Léon's note — "Now is the winter" — how could he possibly have known they were going to kill him?

Plum I doubt he knew that — but I assume he discovered the affair and that was the cause of his "discontent". I suppose the moral is — never trust a woman with a name like Vansittart (*"Fancy tart"*).

Plum heads for the exit, and pauses in the doorway

Ah … Yes … A collective noun for practical jokes! How about — "an exaltation of larks"? Ha, ha! Good-afternoon!

Plum exits

Raymond gives a wry laugh

Raymond Léon used to say to me, "Never forget, the idea of a practical joke is to make people laugh." Nobody laughed at this one, did they?
Sophie Spooky — very spooky!

Curtain

FURNITURE AND PROPERTY LIST

ACT I

On stage: Sofa
Armchairs
Drinks cabinet. *On it*: bottle of mineral water, opened bottle of white
    wine in cooler, bottles of gin, tonic, Scotch, etc.
Table with telephone
Hi-fi and speakers

Off stage: Ice bucket (**Abby**)
Torch and battery-operated storm lamp (**Raymond**)
Candle (**Abby**)
Note (**Raymond**)
Bottle of wine, canapés (**Abby**)
Bottle of port (**Sophie**)

ACT II
SCENE 1

Off stage: Book (**Abby**)
Papers (**Plum**)
Document (**Sergeant**)

Personal: **Plum**: rumpled sheaf of papers including photocopies of two letters

SCENE 2

No additional props

LIGHTING PLOT

Practical fittings required: nil
Interior with exterior backing beyond windows. The same throughout

ACT I

To open: Subdued interior lighting; exterior backing dark

Cue 1	**Abby**: " … thinking of the garden, Mother." *Headlights appear through window; fade*	(Page 5)
Cue 2	**Abby** turns on lights in hall *Bring up lights in hall*	(Page 6)
Cue 3	**Abby**: "… and take it out on me for a week." *Sudden black-out*	(Page 14)
Cue 4	**Abby**: " … it's still simmering gently away." *Headlights through window; fade*	(Page 17)
Cue 5	**John**: "Where does he drag them up from …" *Bring up all lights*	(Page 20)
Cue 6	**John**: "Where's the Scotch?" *Headlights appear though window; fade*	(Page 23)
Cue 7	Second gunshot. **Abby**: "Léon!" *Black-out*	(Page 25)

ACT II, Scene 1

To open: General daytime lighting

Cue 8	**Plum**: " … maiden name was VAN*SIT*TART!" *Black-out*	(Page 40)

ACT II, Scene 2

To open: Same lighting as Scene 1

No cues

EFFECTS PLOT

ACT I

ACT II